Master Class
Play Acting

Written by Ken Ross
Illustrated by Louise Hill

HENDERSON
PUBLISHING PLC

© 1994 Henderson Publishing plc

You're on Stage!

You can be anyone or anything you choose on stage. In the school play or the club panto or just in your front room at home, the theatre stage is a place outside reality. On it, you can be funny or sad, young or old, girl or boy. You can act almost anything. This Master Class book will help you shine. One day, you're bound to find yourself in the spotlight, so here are some tips. Who knows? We might turn a budding young actor or actress into a star!

It's Your Show!.......

We're going to look at some of the skills you need to make your show a success, and we'll look at costumes, stage sets, and at writing the words.

It doesn't matter what you intend to do on stage. It helps if you learn as many basic skills as you can. The way you speak, the way you dress for the part, the way you move, and your facial expressions are all important aspects of your performance.

Starring _____

At Stage Colleges across the world students are taught how to express themselves in all kinds of artistic styles. A student who is a singer may well learn how to move better by having dance lessons. The serious actor may discover fresh ideas for his act by studying comedy.

Whatever you hope to do, by practising different aspects of the performing arts, you will become a more polished performer.

3

An actor's life for me!

Acting comes easily to everyone. As soon as we can talk, as soon as we are aware of people, we begin to act. We play many roles, from a toddler who wishes to attract mum's attention after a fall, to the naughty child who fools his father with an innocent look.

We act in life. Acting on stage is only a short step from reality.

Have you moved my 8mm spanner son?

What's a spanner, Dad?

Try this:

You loaned your favourite pen to these people. How would you ask for its return?

Teacher

Sister

Policeman

Worst enemy

Grandparent

Both your tone of voice, and the words you choose will probably be different in each reply. Maybe you didn't know it, but already you are on the way to becoming a first class performer. And there are other talents you might have that you can use."

Take a positive look at yourself

Can you remember when a parent or a schoolteacher passed you a compliment? What were you doing?
What you were watching on television when you said, 'I can do that!'?
You ARE good at something. You are just as talented as that friend of yours who can play the piano whilst wearing a blindfold.

The hard part is finding what kind of performance best suits your talent. If you can't think what your special talent is, ask those who know you well to suggest one, or read on until you can say, 'Yes, that's me!'.

Music

Can you play an instrument? Besides pianos, violins, guitars and the like, there are home-made instruments. Have you ever filled bottles with different amounts of water, then tapped the bottles with a wooden stick to make musical sounds? Maybe you have twanged elastic bands around a shoe box, or placed a leaf between your thumbs - and your friends have been astonished by your musical gift?

Dance

Don't say you've never tried to boogie.
Or are you the star at the school disco?
There are many kinds of dance. Ballet dancers, tap dancers, modern dancers - all perform on stage. Perhaps you could dance with a partner, or as a group?

Comedy

There are jokers in every class at school. If you know who they are, recruit them for your show or ask them to play a role in your play. If you make people laugh, remember how you do it and put your skills into a comedy act.

Learn as many jokes as you can. Keep rehearsing. The stage is waiting. Everyone wants laughter.

Mime

You don't necessarily need to speak a word. A mime artist needs to be athletic, and to have an eye for detail. Lots of practice in front of a mirror is essential if you are to keep an audience interested.

Can you mime a walk on ice, or a man having a shave? You can portray people's habits or pretend to be a variety of animals.

Impressionist

Can you mimic that funny voice you've heard on television, or sound just like that well known presenter of game shows? An impressionist may also copy mannerisms, facial expressions, or people's dress style. If you have a talent for mimicking what famous people do during their performances - well you're booked!

Singers

Lots of people are blessed with lovely voices. If you're one of them, get learning the songs which bring out the best in your voice.

Even if your voice is terrible, can you make it so comical that people laugh at you? Remember, a singer who has musical friends can form a group.

An Actor's life is not for me

You're not getting out of this so easily. If your show is part of a school project, or a project by you and your many friends, then lots of jobs are on offer.
These are just a few:

Producer

If you're good at organising, then this is for you. Can you get the best out of all those who are taking part? Your performers must know their lines, and they must know where and when to move on stage. You help if things go wrong with any part of the show. You add fresh ideas without causing upset. A producer's job is very important. Qualities needed are a pleasant manner, a sense of responsibility and an ability to think of many things at once.

Stage Manager

The stage manager ensures the smooth running of the performance. Everything must be in the correct place on stage. The performers must know when to enter. Could you cope if the scenery collapsed? Are you quick-thinking and able?

Designer

Have you an eye for scenes which are suitable for the show? A Scene Designer sees to this. Or maybe you have a good dress sense, and you can use your talent as a Costume Designer?

Set Builder

If you're good with your hands, perhaps you can build that pretend wall, or you can make that bench needed for the park scene?

Make-up

Lots of our actors need attention here. We've two lads covered in spots. Can you disguise the spots with make-up? You're hired.
Disguises, too, are a job for our make-up maestro. How good is your imagination? Could you create these disguises? Wicked witch, good fairy, werewolf, elderly Oriental gentleman.
Practise at home with face paints and old clothes.

Jobs and More Jobs

Depending on the number of friends or school pals available, we can offer jobs for:

Wardrobe Assistants
Sound Technicians
Ticket Sellers and Poster Designer
Publicity Director
Programme Sellers
Programme Designers
Lighting Technicians

.... and a host of other things.

Make an application form and get your friends to fill them in. Lay it out something like this:

WANTED

Voluntary workers for the greatest show ever seen. Hours to suit. Terrible pay, -in fact nothing. Bring your own pop and biscuits.

Name:
Address:
Phone No:
Age:
Special talents: i.e.

Acting ___
Singing ___
Dancing ___
Reading ___
Story-telling ___
Costumes ___
Joke-telling ___
Impressions ___
Acrobatics ___
Mime ___
Musical Act ___

Magic ___
Juggling ___
Double Act ___
Poetry ___
Animal Act ___
Make-up ___
Joinery ___
Organisation ___
Design ___
Effects ___
Other (please state)
_____

What would you like to do?
What are you willing to do?
When are you available to meet?

Who's in the audience?

What are the possibilities? Your 75 year old hamster agrees to give you five minutes of its time. You are underwhelmed and invite a few friends around to your house. Your friends cancel and go off to the swimming pool.

You go to the town centre where hundreds of people are walking in the shopping precinct. It rains as it's never rained before. The streets are deserted and you enter an indoor theatre where the manager lets you warm up the crowd. Twenty five million ants crawl out of the stage and frighten the audience away.

The only person remaining is a television show host who gives you a slot on prime-time T.V. You are about to perform in front of half the world's population when..... YOU FREEZE. You've forgotten your lines. Your knees are knocking. You hope the earth will swallow you up.

Aren't you relieved when Morris, the hamster nibbles at your toes and wakes you from the dream? Your audience can be anyone, but its best to keep the bigger audiences until you are ready.

So let's make a modest start.

Where is our stage?

A school project is ideal as most schools possess a stage. Clubs and organisations usually have an area which can be used by artistes. But is there a stage in your house? No? Then let's make use of what we can find for the moment. Here are three ideas:

Your bedroom is the ideal room for a first performance to friends.

For a little more space to move about, turn your lawn into an open-air theatre - or use the local park.

The garage could be the very place you need. Clear a space and invite your friends to watch the show.

We're ready for practice

Our small area is ready. We're probably alone, or with our dearest friend who's going to giggle the moment we do anything dramatic. But when the roles are reversed, and they make a fool of themselves, then we can giggle too. If you are alone, put a cuddly toy on a chair in front of you and pretend it is your audience.

Wherever your stage is, when you are performing, choose a focal point in the audience, and play to that focal point. As you improve, you will need this focal point increasingly less.

Nervous yet?

Here are some ideas for exercises that will build up your confidence. Don't be content to do them once. When you've completed one exercise, think how you can improve your performance, then do it again.

1. Speak about yourself. Try to make your life interesting. Talk about your hobbies, your holidays, your friends, your prize possessions. Put your feelings into the speech. Use the best words you can think of, and use your hands to add expression.

2. Read aloud an extract from a book or from a story. Put feeling into the words. Make your voice reflect the meaning of the words and allow it to rise and fall with the flow of the sentence.

3. Think of a character. Your character either loves or hates his or her neighbours. Try to make your audience of one feel just as your character does about the neighbours.

4. If you can find the lyrics of a song, sing the song in as many different voices as you can. Sing the song miserably, then sing it happily. Use your imagination, try to perform this piece in a variety of ways. You will discover ways that work well and ways that don't work at all.

Nothing is working - 'I'm shy'...

Morris the hamster has been your audience and you can't even fight your blushes to perform for him. Oh, dear.

You put Morris on stage and you become his audience. But Morris is even worse than you. Tell him so. Play the part of a heckler.

'I'm 75 years old,' says Morris. 'Just watch me!'

Speak out. Say what you think about Morris's act. Strike up a dialogue with Morris even though he's not answering you.

TIPS:
* Try to get something going.
* Try to get used to the sound of your own voice.
* Concentrate on you and your world of make-believe.
* If you keep practising, the thought will eventually arrive that there was something good in what you have just done.

Voice Training

You're coming along fine. Your best friend has stopped giggling and all your neighbours are wearing ear-plugs to block out the sound of the crazy kids next door. Only joking!

You are beginning to believe that the Greatest Show Ever Seen could attract a big audience.

But will the crowd hear you? Can you project your voice?

When on stage, it is not enough to speak in your normal tone.

lounge (you) kitchen (a friend)

Try this

Indoors, send your friend into the next room. When your friend is out of sight, begin talking and ask the friend to respond.
Don't shout, and don't call, 'You what? I didn't hear you.'
Simply make your voice louder by degrees, until it is powerful enough to be heard. Practise this technique until you are able to speak in a louder tone without appearing to shout. It's a useful skill to develop, although quiet types will find it uncomfortable at first.

Clarity

Can your audience understand what you are saying? One of your lines is:

'The butter had better not melt in the heat of the sun.'

Suppose you mumbled the line, and you did not speak clearly. The audience might hear you say: 'The bu'er'd ber'er no mel in the he of the sun.'

Let's pronounce our t's and our h's. Let's sing the song or speak the line as the writer heard it in his head.

> **TIP:**
>
> Recite these tongue-twisters until you can deliver them perfectly:
> * Roger Grainger's dangerous drain flooded in Dufton Drive.
> * Brother Hubbard had bother bathing his bruises on Brighton beach.
> * Dancer Daphne's dainty daughter fell and fainted on the path.
> * About half-way, Horris injured his abdomen.
> * She's seen shocking scenes of Samantha Scarlet screaming.

Delivery

John Kennedy, who was once president of the United States of America, often spoke at a rate of hundreds of words per minute. To become a president is not our intention. To become a play actor or actress, you need to speak at a much slower rate. You must deliver your words at a pace which each member of the audience will hear clearly.

Example 1:

(read speedily until you come to the full stop)

'Good evening ladies and gentlemen my name is Hiram Tonsil lead singer of the Fabulous Flabbies and tonight we would like to perform our number one hit Wobbling All Over Mars.'

Example 2:

(pause at the end of each line)
'Good evening, ladies and gentlemen.
My name is Hiram Tonsil, lead singer of the Fabby Flabbies.
Tonight, we would like to perform our number one hit, Wobbling All Over Mars.'
How much clearer was the second delivery? Can you divide a paragraph into shorter lines that will improve your delivery?

> **TIP:**
> **Speak,**
>   **Pause,**
>   **Breathe**
> ....and your lines will be clearer.

Learning to move - let your body talk

Can you imagine going to see a performance where everyone stands still on stage? Suffering statues! That *would* be boring. They'd look like lots of trees on a windless day and the audience would soon go home.

So let's practise moving. Find out what these words mean if you don't already know.

Get Morris the hamster to watch you do these actions and, if you feel you can, try to put words to your movements.

COWER GRUMBLE TREMBLE RUSH SHIVER SNARL FIGHT DEFEND RELAX AWAKE SLEEP ENQUIRE SHOCK CREEP ENCOUNTER

It would be very difficult not to move. Even sleepers move.

Move your arms

Move your legs

Relax - don't be stiff

Watch your back

Movement on stage adds to the performance. But remember, the audience *does not wish to see your back*. Try and face the audience as much as possible.

> **TIPS:**
> * Watch television shows. How do the actors move?
> * What do singers do to make their performances come alive?
> * If you are able to visit a theatre, watch everything that goes on.
> * If your stage is 5 metres wide - try to make use of it all, not just the width of your shoes!

Don't be afraid to touch each other

Get in close

Standing behind is okay, so long as your face is showing

GESTICULATE - use your hands!

Get distant

Look like a crackpot!

After all your hard work, you deserve a really good laugh. It's time to look in the mirror and to discover an elastic face.

Words, songs, movements all have meaning. If the expression on your face matches the meaning, then WOW! - you're on your way to some epic play acting.

Look in the mirror. Remember, you've got eyes, eyebrows, lips, teeth, and a jaw. Show these expressions, and any more you can think of:

ANGER LOVE HAPPY SAD DOUBT PUZZLED NERVOUS TIRED SILLY SURPRISE STUPID BORED THINKING EXCITED CUNNING

Does your face ache now? It may do if you've worked very hard.

"What's wrong, pal?"

"I've been acting!"

Learning Lines

75 years old. He's seen it all, done it all, but ......Morris never learned how to read. He can't help you.

If your friend is willing to help, then learning lines is much easier. Take it in turns to read out the words. Gradually stop looking at the book and you'll soon find a few sentences being remembered. Ask your friend to prompt you when you can't recall the next bit.

So, we need to rehearse. We need to say the lines over and over again until we know them by heart.

How did mum teach you that first nursery rhyme? How come you know the words of many pop songs? By saying them over and over again.

You can do it. It's as easy as learning your name and address.

Lines as pictures

Try learning these few lines. See how long it takes you before you can recite them without looking:

"Cynthia, will you go to the shop?
The shop on the corner.
I've ordered two magazines.
The Shoe Repairer, and The Hat Designer.
Will you collect them, please?"

Challenge

This is a important method to help you learn lines, piece by piece. Now find a book or magazine and choose a piece of monologue (one person's speech). Try to learn it with pictures in your mind, until you can say the whole paragraph aloud without looking. If you succeed, that's a good start.

TIP:

It can help if you visualise what is going on in the words. Picture Cynthia going to the corner shop, then looking down at the magazines. Then think of your shoes and a hat on your head.

Putting it all together with Voice, Movement and Expression

Stand in front of the biggest mirror you can find and try out these performances:

You are:

| The meanest person on earth | A singer in a comedy | A young person in love |

Your Lines:

Make up some characters. Try to feel as they feel. Try to say the words that they might say.

"Darling, my heart beats rapidly, my hopes are higher than mountains,
my future may be filled with joy if .....
if you say you will be mine.'

'My name is Jake Band.
I'm like a snake.
I slither and I dither
I crawl and fall
I turn on soil
I'm out in rotten weather.'

Give you money? I've saved, I've struggled, I've gone without every luxury known to humankind. I shan't give you a coin!'

Using a tape recorder

It's amazing how many people hear their voices on a tape recording, and are surprised how they sound. Regional accents, peculiarities of speech, *hums* and *aarghs*, are all picked up by the recorder. We are not so aware of them during our everyday conversations. We know how people we meet sound, but we don't usually hear our own voice.

If you have a machine that can record your voice, then use the microphone and practise some exercises earlier in the book. You may improve your delivery, or your pronunciation. You never know, you may be quite pleased with how you do sound.

Challenge:
Try to use different voices. Practise an old person's voice. Imitate a strong accent. Copy the voice of a newsreader on the TV. or a D.J.

Half-way to Stardom

We have dealt with lots of areas which, with practice, will improve your performance. Whether you intend to sing, or you wish to act in the Greatest Show Ever Seen, you will get better and better each time you rehearse.

The old saying, 'practice makes perfect', is true. The people we see on our television screens, and those we see in films, have worked very hard to achieve their high standards.

But there is more needed.

Our stage can be anything from a simple soapbox, to...

To make our performance work well, we need a stage and all its accessories.

The Stage
The Backcloth

The backcloth, or backdrop, is what we see behind the actors. It is sometimes a scene painted on wooden boards. This scene can be of a city, of countryside, of a room. It can be virtually what you want it to be. But unless you are an artist, or have artistic friends, then we'll have to look at some simpler ideas.

country or garden - create this easily with paper or paints.

You can use large pieces of paper stuck together. If you change colours about, or make a variety of paper shapes, you will get many different effects. Choose the effect that goes best with your type of act. If you were singing a song about sunshine and birds, then yellow curtains and cut out paper birds would create the scene.

seascape - an impression of the sea is all you need to give to set the scene.

unreal landscape - a wierd and powerful effect comes about with strange colour and shapes.

use bright colours and paper shapes, pinned to old bed sheets or curtains for ideal backcloths.

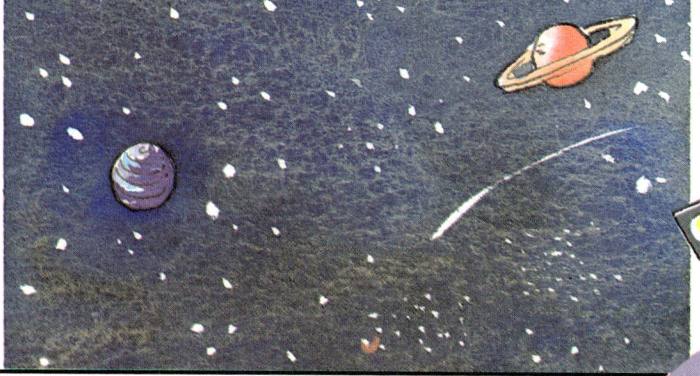

spacescape - use newspapers to cut and stick large collage scenes. Then paint what you like.

Props

If we use a backcloth, then we should use stage props which do not seem out of place. The scenes we used for our backcloths are much improved if we put one of the following items on our stage:

Props should be improvised. This means you don't have to find the real thing, like a rocket, or a spinning wheel. You can create the impression of that item with clever paper craft.

Do you know which prop we should use for each backcloth, or backdrop, on the previous page?

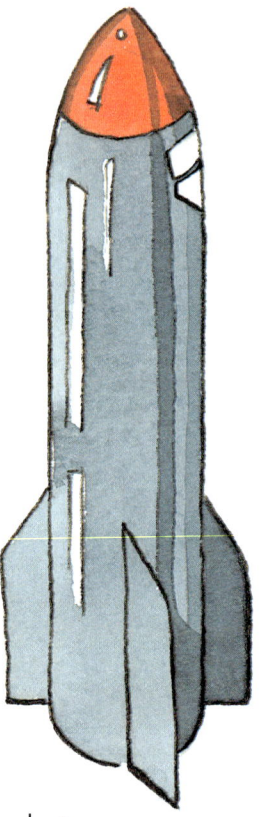

a rocket

a sandy-coloured carpet

a black boulder

a bench

Try to match the overall theme of your performance with your stage props.
It is a bit like choosing the right outfit for the right occasion.

Here are some ideas for things you can use:
Keep a look out for good props you can borrow. Don't clutter your stage. A clever prop is one which sets the scene. A single item can determine the period in which your play is set. A spinning wheel, for example, clearly shows you are not in a modern scene.

You can make stage items, or props, out of cardboard boxes:

* cover and scatter boxes with green cloth to create a grassy landscape
* if grey cloth is used, then you might have a mountain side
* yellow cloth would suggest sand dunes

> **Challenge**
> Imagine a scene; a man is walking his dog. Which props would you choose? Which would suit a murder mystery play?

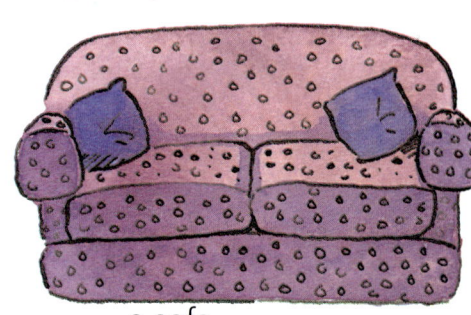

a small zebra crossing

a sofa

a painting

a street light

Paint cardboard boxes to make drawers, suitcases, pillar boxes, safes, chests and anything else you can imagine.

a cardboard dog

a telephone

Get a pair of scissors and experiment in prop design. Always keep in mind the mood of the performance for which you are making props.

Where to find stage props

Most items you will need can be found in the house, or can be made. So don't go spending all your savings on something you may only use once.

If you use your imagination, you can make almost anything with cardboard boxes from your local supermarket. Bottles, jars, plastic containers, pieces of wood can all be used.

Here are some things made from cardboard boxes.

Costumes

It's fun dressing up. If you look dressed for the occasion it will also make you feel more fitting for the part.

Costumes should also reflect the type of act you do. A tap dancer wouldn't wear a shawl and a long black skirt, and a rock singer would hardly be seen dressed as a nun.

Make your costume fit the part. The better you feel in your costume, the more likely you will perform well.

Where to find costumes

* Ask your granny, or some other kindly relative, for any unwanted clothes.
* Can you make any hats from boxes and bags?
* Have you looked in charity shops?
* Have you ever seen the huge amount of old clothes at jumble sales, or at church sales?
* And what about car boot sales? Again, don't go spending your savings. Tell the seller that you've only got a small amount of money. You will probably pick up your costume for the price of a few packets of sweets - and you'll be amazed what you find to make up some really effective costumes.

What makes a good costume?

In one word - IMAGINATION.
Try to make your costume a little larger than life. Make that hat a fraction bigger than usual. Make that buttonhole flower more stunning than a real flower. If you're a comedian, have your jacket too big, or too small. If you're a singer, don't just look smart, look startling!

Costumes should be more obvious than clothes worn in ordinary life. You are playing a make-believe role. If you convince your audience that you really look like this extraordinary character, they will be impressed by your performance even before you have spoken.

Off-stage items

You may need make-up and a change of costume. It is sensible to practise using make-up if it is to be part of your stage role. Ask mum if she has an old lipstick or an old powder puff she can donate to your wardrobe. If you do need to change costume, make sure your second costume is laid out off stage.
A quick change may be essential. It is not a good idea to keep your audience waiting.

Special Effects

Special effects can also be conducted off stage. You will need someone to create an atmosphere during your performance, or to make a pretend snake rush across your feet. These special effects need rehearsing too.

Here are some ideas. Can you think of any more?

- whistling - the wind, or something scary

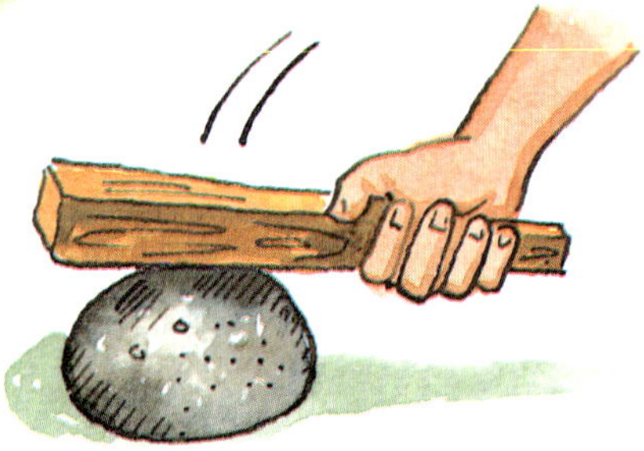

- wood tapped on stone - footsteps

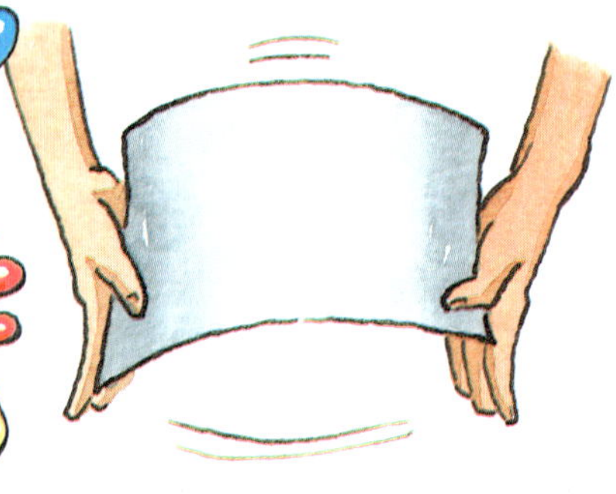

- wobbling board - to make thunderclaps

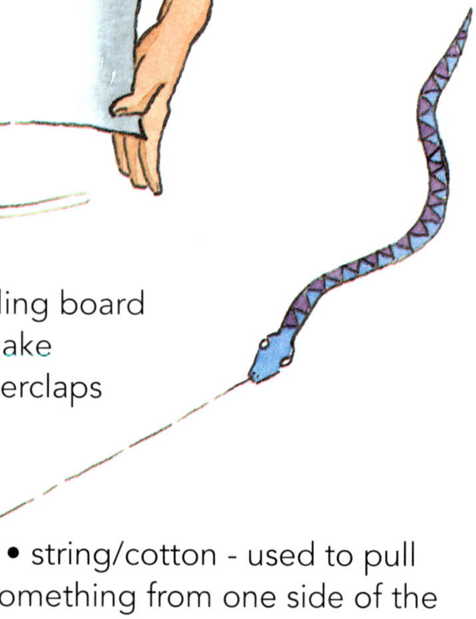

- string/cotton - used to pull something from one side of the stage to the other

- musical instrument - to build an atmosphere, or to introduce a new sequence of events

- tins crashing - haunted house effect, car crash

- alarm clock - security bell

- twigs cracking - something is threatening

- newspaper torn/ruffled - movement of the unknown

Challenge

Almost anything you pick up can produce a sound. Experiment, see how many different noises you can make. Some of the noises may inspire an idea for a play.

The Performer's Script

However well we can act or sing, and whatever we look like on stage, our performance can't go ahead without words. Even mime artists, musicians, acrobats and silent magicians have the outline of their acts written down.

We need words for the singer in a song lyric. We need words for the comedian in the jokes. And for the actor, words make up a play.

Write it yourself

If you have a favourite poem, joke, story or quotation, perfect this and use it in your act. Don't stick to other people's words - try to create some of your own.
Write a funny short story, or recite a poem you have written. Original material delivered with feeling will interest any audience.

1. Walking the elevator
2. Climbing a ladder
3. Trying the locked door
4. Stroking a bird

1. Song: "Imagine"
2. Song: "Let it be"
3. Anecdote - journey to theatre
4. Song: "All my Loving"

Trick with eggs
- then egg cups
Trick with knives and forks
Table cloth trick
- disappearing table

Chorus:
Can't you find a way
Can't you find a way to love me
Maybe one day
You will find your way

Joke:
What's black and white and red all over?

A sunburnt zebra.

Samantha:
(leaning forward and snatching the parcel from Godfrey)
It's mine!

Get your idea down

If you have a spare notebook, then use it for writing down your ideas. One day you may have an idea for a song, but the idea is insufficient for you to write a whole lyric. If you write down the idea, then sometime later you may be able to work on it again. The idea is not lost in your head.

As you fill up your notebook with ideas, you will find it easier to write more and more works. Here is an example:

Note 1: You return from holiday on the train and think a song that imitates the sound of a train would be original.

Note 3: You read about a super new express train that is going to be the fastest in the world.

Note 2: You think of the line, 'The train arriving on Platform 3...'

If you put these ideas together, you can write a song lyric about waiting to return from holiday on the world's fastest train. The refrain (the line or verse repeated several times) is 'The train arriving on Platform 3...' and the tune imitates the sound of a very fast train.

Funny Ideas

The only comedians who don't want to hear a new joke are bad comedians and dead comedians. So if comedy is your forte, then jot down every funny incident and joke you hear about. A good new joke is very precious. Some very famous comedians pay lots of money for good new jokes.

You can make jokes up, you can steal them from other funny people, but you need to know *many* jokes before you can put together a five minute act.
Put your jokes in categories. Record all the jokes about elephants separately to all the jokes about monkeys.

Example: You have three jokes about elephants, four jokes about monkeys, and two jokes about headless monsters. You remember these nine jokes by remembering these keys words.

elephant / trunk / shoes / chimp

monkey / roller skates / ice cream / lost his head

headless monster / house / mother

Your comedy routine may go something like this:
'Elephants, now they're funny creatures. I saw Mr. and Mrs. Elephant go into a seaside shop - they bought a pair of trunks. And there's another elephant I know who takes a size 95 shoe - that's without socks on. He's got a chimp as a friend - I call them Hunky and Monkey.'

'Talking about monkeys - heard about the monkey owner called Guy Riller? His monkey bought some roller skates to go on holiday - it went to Chimp-On-Sea. The monkey brought me an ice cream back, we shared it - a banana split. But it fell in love with another monkey. It lost it's head, never seen it since.'

'I've seen a headless monster though. In my house. I said, 'Where you heading off to?' 'To my mother's,' it said. But I didn't see it's lips move.'

Each joke should introduce the next joke. Keep them flowing and try to tell a continuous story. Even if some humour is lost when you join jokes together, your audience will be involved in the story.

Can you list all the funny incidents and jokes you know, then arrange them so that one item flows into the next?

Challenge

In which order would you tell these jokes?

Play Writing

Before we attempt to write our masterpiece, we must first know just how many of our friends are going to take part in The Greatest Show Ever Seen.

If you know no-one who is willing, then a one person play is what you should do.

- Include only as few characters as possible.
- Have as few stage sets as possible.
- Think about the stage sets and the costumes you can obtain before attempting to write your play.

Try this:

Scene: wood backcloth, or backdrop, with mystery parcel
Actors: you and a friend
Costumes: a woodcutter and a witch

challenge

Write a short scene that makes use of the scene, the costumes, and two actors.

What should you have in a play?

In one word - DRAMA!
Our play should have a beginning, middle, and ending, but if it hasn't got drama, then the audience may not stay to see them all.

Grip 'em

If our play began like this, would you stay to watch the ending?

Mr. Smith (sitting): Hello. Nice day today.

Mr. Ball (sitting): Yes. A very nice day.

Mr. Smith: Thought I'd go for a stroll.

Mr. Ball: Me too.

No Way! Half the audience would have fallen asleep or reached for a tomato to throw at messieurs Smith and Ball. But if we began like this:

Mr. Smith (running on stage): Quick, she's hurt.
Mr. Ball : Did you see them?
Mr. Smith (pointing): There were two, in masks. They took the box.

Wow! Who is hurt? Who did Mr. Smith see? Why were they wearing masks? What is in the box?

Would you leave the theatre at this point? You'd be on the edge of your seat waiting for the next dramatic moment.

A play, then, is filled with dramatic moments and action. To keep your audience interested you must make the story move.

Can you write two small parts which are both interesting, and filled with action?

Here are some ideas. You can choose two characters, a scene, and what has happened, or you can think of your own.

CHARACTERS	SCENE	WHAT'S HAPPENED
Shopkeeper	Classroom	An injury
Policeman	Graveyard	Something is lost
Farmer	Shop	Something is found
Lost person	Footpath	One person has lied
Knowall	Field	The hottest day ever
Very rich person	Ruin	One person is scared
Schoolteacher	Church	They've long lost friends
Bodyguard	Mountain top	They hate each other
Vicar	Prison cell	A secret is told
Nurse	Fun fair	They are trapped
Thief	Beach	One person is deaf
Good Samaritan	Wood	They're both starving
Dreamer	Tiny room	They're saying goodbye
Argumentative type	Ledge	One's witnessed a disaster
Angel	Cave	They've fallen in love
Demon	Car	One person is shrinking
Ghost	Waiting room	One person is hypnotised

Use Natural Dialogue

If you read the script of a play you will notice that the language is slightly different to the text of a book. What we like to read is slightly different from the style of language we speak everyday.

So when you write a line of dialogue, say it aloud first.
Ask yourself if it trips naturally off the tongue.
Listen to people talking - notice how what they say might look odd if written down.

Take this piece of actual speech:
'No, I can't... I don't think I can. I don't know. We'll just have to see how I do.'

It both looks and reads very unnaturally, but if you say the words aloud, it becomes clear that this is a natural reply that echoes a person's self doubt. Perhaps a doctor has asked a man with a stiff back to take off his shoes and touch his toes.

Dialogue should always be easy to say. It doesn't matter what it looks like on paper.

Characterisation

Have you ever heard it said that, 'He's a right character'? Usually the person is larger than life, a complete individual whom you wouldn't mistake in a crowd. Well, that's what your characters should be. Give each character something unique - make your characters memorable. Exaggerate them.

Here are some ideas:

- the woman who is forever pointing her finger

- the boy with purple and green hair

- the man with the biggest smile in the world

- the man who jerks his head after every few words

- the girl who speaks very, very slowly

- the girl who uses the word 'fantastic' to describe everything

- the boy who can't ever sit still

See if you can add something to your characters that will make them larger than life. Don't worry if their habit gets on your nerves - some people really do!

43

Sample Plays

The Birdie

(Comedy sketch for one actor)

Scene: Woodland and cottage interior

Actor is standing in a wood wearing a huge smile and enjoying the natural surroundings. When:

Sound effect: loud bang

Actor jumps with surprise, loses balance and falls over.

The actor fumbles with something on the ground.

Actor: (rising to feet after picking up wounded bird): What are nasty, nasty men with shotguns doing shooting a lovely, lovely birdie like you?

The actor cuddles the bird, inspects its damaged wing, then he cradles it in his arms.

Actor: You need protection. I will take you home with me where it is warm.

The actor goes behind the central curtain.

Sound effect: commotion, banging, squealing.

The actor appears in the home side of the stage carrying an upturned cardboard box on a tray.

He sits at table, lifts the box to reveal a pie with bird's wings protruding from the crust. He rubs a knife and fork together and smiles wickedly at the audience.

The Safe Crackers

(sketch for two actors)

Scene: office with table, chair and safe. Actor 2 is attempting to unlock the safe while Actor 1 keeps watch.

Actor 1: There's only a few minutes left.

Actor 2: I'm doing my best. Don't bug me.

Actor 1: She'll be back soon... hurry.

Actor 2: What do you think I'm doing - admiring the craftsmanship?

Actor 1: You know what will happen if we don't crack the combination?

Actor 2: Sure, I know.

Actor 1: You know how long we'll have to wait?

Actor 2: Sure, sure. I need them as much as you. I was late out of bed - never had time...

Actor 1: There's only a minute or so before...

Actor 2: Ssh! Ssh! (puts ear to the safe, listens while turning the dial)
Ha, cracked it!

Actor 1: (rubbing hands in delight) Great stuff!

Actor 2: (taking a plate of sandwiches from inside safe and inspecting their contents) Well... ham salad or cheese and pickle?

All ready to go

We've come a long way. It's about time we got our show on the road. Here is a plan for you to follow that will make the preparation easier. Try not to rush. The more attention you give to detail, the better your show will be.

A: Decide what kind of performance is for you.
ACTOR / SINGER / DANCER / COMEDIAN
MUSICIAN / OTHER

B: Decide what script/music/routine you are going to use.
WRITE IT YOURSELF / YOU ALREADY KNOW IT / CHOOSE ONE FROM A BOOK OR MUSICAL SORE

C: Where are you going to perform?
HOME / GARDEN / GARAGE / SCHOOL / CLUB / OTHER

D: Where is the stage area?
MAKE ONE / ALREADY EXISTS

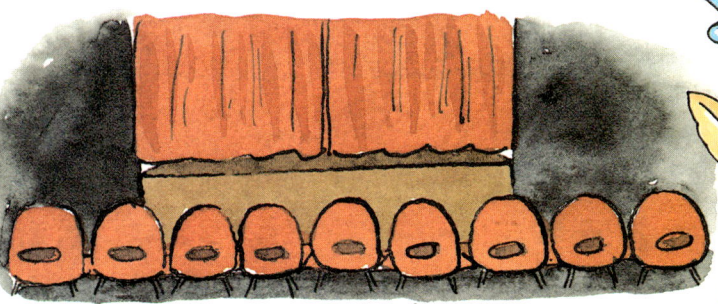

E: What stage set is needed for your performance?
BACKCLOTH / SET FURNITURE / ITEMS USED IN PERFORMANCE

F: Decide which costume/costumes you are going to wear.

G: Who is going to attend your performance?
FRIENDS / RELATIVES / SCHOOL MATES / NEIGHBOURS / OTHERS

H: When is your performance to take place?

Break a leg! as they say in the theatre for good luck!

The Finale

You can do it!

Yes you can. If you want to entertain people, whether by acting, singing, dancing, or even writing plays, you can do it. It is not impossible for you to make a career as a performer.

If you look back on your very first attempt at performing, you will probably think it wasn't very good. You will think how much improved your present level of performance is by comparison.

Well, go on improving, go on asking how you can get better and better. Rehearse. Be determined that your next performance will be the best yet.

Determination to improve brings results in the end. If you got over your friend's giggles, then you can get over other obstacles too.

Say to yourself, 'I can do it!' Who knows, one day we might be watching you on T.V. And what will your giggling friend say then....?